BENJAMIN BRITTEN

REJOICE IN THE LAMB

*Festival Cantata
for Chorus (SATB)
with Treble, Alto, Tenor and Bass solos,
and Organ*

Op. 30

Words by
Christopher Smart

BOOSEY & HAWKES

AN IMAGEM COMPANY

DISTRIBUTED BY

HAL•LEONARD®
CORPORATION
7777 W. BLUEMOUND RD. P.O. BOX 13819 MILWAUKEE, WI 53213

www.boosey.com
www.halleonard.com

REJOICE IN THE LAMB
Op. 30

Festival Cantata for Chorus (SATB) with Treble, Alto, Tenor and Bass solos, and Organ. Composed May–17 July 1943. Text by Christopher Smart. First published by Boosey & Hawkes in 1943.

Dedication: "For the Rev. Walter Hussey and the choir of St. Matthew's Church, Northampton, on the occasion of the 50th anniversary of the consecration of their church, September 21st 1943."

First performance: 21 September 1943, St. Matthew's Church, Northampton, England. Choir of St. Matthew's Church, Northampton, Charles Barker (organ), Benjamin Britten (conductor).

First broadcast: 31 October 1943, BBC Home Service. Choir of St. Matthew's Church, Northampton, Benjamin Britten (conductor).

Duration: 16 minutes

Available orchestration: Imogen Holst's orchestration, written at the request of Benjamin Britten for a concert given at the 1952 Aldeburgh Festival. Scored for small orchestra, it realizes the orchestral colors latent in the more familiar organ version with great skill and imagination.

Available on rental from Boosey & Hawkes.

Other Britten compositions from this period: *Now sleeps the crimson petal* (Tenor, Horn and Strings, completed 22 March 1943); Serenade, Op. 31 (Tenor, Horn and Strings, March–April 1943); Prelude and Fugue, Op. 29 (18-part String Orchestra, May 1943); *The Rescue* (incidental music to the radio drama, September–November 1943); *The Ballad of Little Musgrave and Lady Barnard* (Male Voices and Piano, completed 13 December 1943). [1]

*   *   *   *   *   *   *

Printed in U.S.A. and distributed by Hal Leonard Corporation, Milwaukee WI

It was in 1937 that Rev. Walter Hussey, then Vicar of St. Matthew's Church, Northampton, and later Dean of Chichester Cathedral had the idea of bringing artists and the Church back together — something extraordinary in England at that time. "How sad it was," he said, "that the arts had become largely divorced from the Church: Sad, because artists think and meditate a lot and are in the broadest sense of the word 'religious'. They create fine expressions of the human spirit which can symbolize and express worship, as well as conveying the truth of God to mankind in a vivid and memorable way."

Hussey began to think about the 50th anniversary of the consecration of St. Matthew's Church and his desire to "get a piece of music written for the occasion." He wrote to Benjamin Britten in March, 1943: "I have been wondering whether you would consider the possibility of a commission to write some music for our Jubilee celebrations next September — perhaps a four-part anthem for our voluntary choir of men's and boys' voices. I have had a great 'bee' about a closer connection between the Church and the arts." Britten responded that he "also had a 'bee' about a closer connection between the arts and the Church and am thinking about something lively for such an occasion." [2]

Interestingly, the piece was begun shortly thereafter (in May) and completed in July, 1943. The poem which Britten chose, "Rejoice in the Lamb" by Christopher Smart is a long poem from which Britten selected certain parts totaling 10 sections. Smart, an 18th-century poet in whom genius and madness were nearly together, was practically unknown at that time. The theme is 'Benedicite Omnia opera' with some of God's humblest creations being called upon to testify to the glory of God. When Hussey expressed reservations about the 'cat' section, Britten replied: "I've used a bit about the cat Jeffrey, but don't see how it could hurt anyone — he is such a nice cat." *The Times* of London reviewed the concert and felt that 'the spirit of the curious, vivid poem has been caught and the outcome of a commission by the Church for a modern work of religious art' is beautiful.

The title, "Rejoice in the Lamb" is the same that Smart used, only his was in Latin — "Jubilate Agno." The title comes from a passage in the book of Revelation: "Salvation to our God which sitteth upon the throne, and unto the Lamb." Smart wanted "Jubilate Agno" to be closely parallel to portions of the Order for Morning Prayer and the Psalter and was intended as a responsive reading, which is why the Let and For sections are physically distinct while corresponding verse for verse. He was admitted to St. Luke's Hospital for the insane in 1757 and "Jubilate Agno" was begun after this time and took four years to complete, the last line being written on 30 January 1763 very near the date of Smart's release from a second asylum.

Britten came to St. Matthew's and conducted final rehearsals and the premiere. He later wrote to Rev. Hussey: "I do hope that I have given you something which will be of more lasting value than just for this particular occasion." And, indeed, he had!

— Philip Brunelle

[1] *Benjamin Britten: Britten: A Catalogue of the Published Works,*
  compiled and edited by Paul Banks
  (Aldeburgh: published by The Britten-Pears Library for the Britten Estate Limited, 1999), 65 – 69

[2] *Letters from a Life: Selected Letters and Diaries of Benjamin Britten*
  Volume Two 1939 – 45
  edited by Donald Mitchell and Philip Reed
  (London: Faber and Faber Limited, 1991), 1139, 1142, 1143, 1157, 1161, 1162

NOTE FROM THE ORIGINAL PUBLICATION

The words of the Cantata – "Rejoice in the Lamb" – are taken from a long poem of the same name. The writer was Christopher Smart, an eighteenth century poet, deeply religious, but of a strange and unbalanced mind.

"Rejoice in the Lamb" was written while Smart was in an asylum, and is chaotic in form but contains many flashes of genius.

It is a few of the finest passages that Benjamin Britten has chosen to set to music. The main theme of the poem, and that of the Cantata, is the worship of God, by all created beings and things, each in its own way.

The Cantata is made up of ten short sections. The first sets the theme. The second gives a few examples of one person after another being summoned from the pages of the Old Testament to join with some creature in praising and rejoicing in God. The third is a quiet and ecstatic Hallelujah. In the fourth section Smart takes his beloved cat as an example of nature praising God by being simply what the Creator intended it to be. The same thought is carried on in the fifth section with the illustration of the mouse. The sixth section speaks of the flowers – "the poetry of Christ." In the seventh section Smart refers to his troubles and suffering, but even these are an occasion for praising God, for it is through Christ that he will find his deliverance. The eighth section gives four letters from an alphabet, leading to a full chorus in section nine which speaks of musical instruments and music's praise of God. The final section repeats the Hallelujah.

— Walter Hussey

* * * * * * *

Text from *Jubilate Agno* by Christopher Smart

CHORUS
Rejoice in God, O ye Tongues; give the glory to the Lord, and the Lamb.
Nations, and languages, and every Creature, in which is the breath of Life.
Let man and beast appear before him, and magnify his name together.
Let Nimrod, the mighty hunter, bind a Leopard to the altar, and consecrate his spear to the Lord.
Let Ishmael dedicate a Tyger, and give praise for the liberty in which the Lord has let him at large.
Let Balaam appear with an Ass, and bless the Lord his people and his creatures for a reward eternal.
Let Daniel come forth with a Lion, and praise God with all his might through faith in Christ Jesus.
Let Ithamar minister with a Chamois, and bless the name of Him, that cloatheth the naked.
Let Jakim with the Satyr bless God in the dance.
Let David bless with the Bear – The beginning of victory to the Lord – to the Lord the perfection of excellence – Hallelujah from the heart of God, and from the hand of the artist inimitable, and from the echo of the heavenly harp in sweetness magnifical and mighty.

TREBLE SOLO

For I will consider my cat Jeoffry.

For he is the servant of the Living God, duly and daily serving him.

For at the first glance of the glory of God in the East he worships in his way.

For this is done by wreathing his body seven times round with elegant quickness.

For he knows that God is his Saviour.

For God has blessed him in the variety of his movements.

For there is nothing sweeter than his peace when at rest.

For I am possessed of a cat, surpassing in beauty, from whom I take occasion to bless Almighty God.

ALTO SOLO

For the Mouse is a creature of great personal valour.

For – this a true case – Cat takes female mouse – male mouse will not depart, but stands threat'ning and daring.

...If you will let her go, I will engage you, as prodigious a creature as you are.

For the Mouse is a creature of great personal valour.

For the Mouse is of an hospitable disposition.

TENOR SOLO

For the flowers are great blessings.

For the flowers have their angels even the words of God's Creation.

For the flower glorifies God and the root parries the adversary.

For there is a language of flowers.

For flowers are peculiarly the poetry of Christ.

CHORUS

For I am under the same accusation with my Saviour –

For they said, he is besides himself.

For the officers of the peace are at variance with me, and the watchman smites me with his staff.

For Silly fellow! Silly fellow! is against me and belongeth neither to me nor to my family.

For I am in twelve HARDSHIPS, but he that was born of a virgin shall deliver me out of all.

RECITATIVE (BASS SOLO) AND CHORUS

For H is a spirit and therefore he is God.

For K is king and therefore he is God.

For L is love and therefore he is God.

For M is musick and therefore he is God.

For the instruments are by their rhimes.

For the Shawm rhimes are lawn fawn moon boon and the like.

For the harp rhimes are sing ring string and the like.

For the cymbal rhimes are bell well toll soul and the like.

For the flute rhimes are tooth youth suit mute and the like.

For the Bassoon rhimes are pass class and the like.

For the dulcimer rhimes are grace place beat heat and the like.

For the Clarinet rhimes are clean seen and the like.

For the trumpet rhimes are sound bound soar more and the like.

For the TRUMPET of God is a blessed intelligence and so are all the instruments in HEAVEN.

For GOD the father Almighty plays upon the HARP of stupendous magnitude and melody.

For at that time malignity ceases and the devils themselves are at peace.

For this time is perceptible to man by a remarkable stillness and serenity of soul.

CHORUS

Hallelujah from the heart of God, and from the hand of the artist inimitable, and from the echo of the heavenly harp in sweetness magnifical and mighty.

For the Rev. Walter Hussey and the choir of St. Matthew's Church, Northampton, on the occasion of the 50th anniversary of the consecration of their church, September 21st 1943

REJOICE IN THE LAMB
Festival Cantata

CHRISTOPHER SMART

BENJAMIN BRITTEN
Op. 30

lan - gua - ges, _____ and e - ver - y Crea - ture in which is the

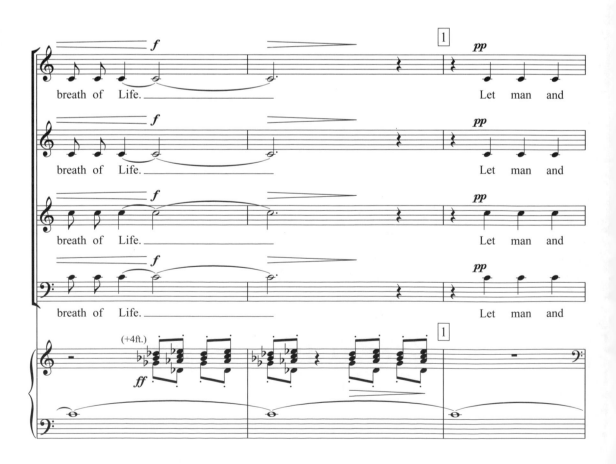

breath of Life. _____ Let man and

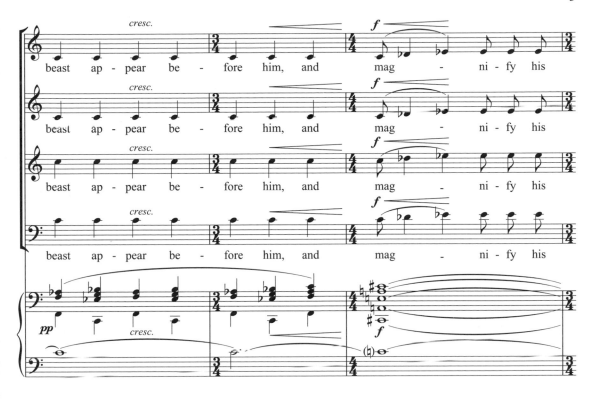

beast ap - pear be - fore him, and mag - ni - fy his

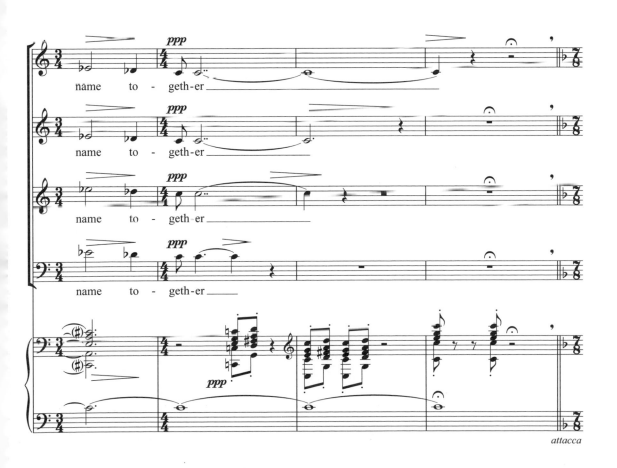

name to - geth-er

attacca

4

With vigour (♪ = 200)
(*Con brio*)

With vigour (♪ = 200)
(*Con brio*)

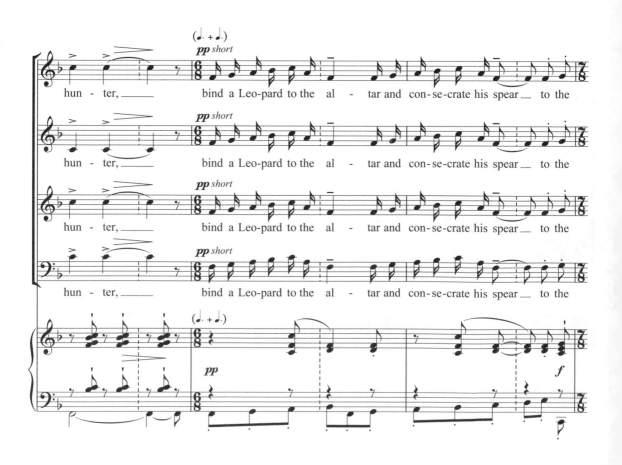

8

Cha-mois, and bless the name of Him that cloath-eth the

Cha-mois, and bless the name of Him that cloath-eth the

Cha-mois, and bless the name of Him that cloath-eth the

Cha-mois, and bless the name of Him that cloath-eth the

na - ked. Let Ja - kim with the Sa - tyr.

na - ked. Let Ja - kim with the Sa - tyr.

na - ked. Let Ja - kim with the Sa - tyr.

na - ked. Let Ja - kim with the Sa - tyr.

10

9 **Gently moving** (♩ = 60)
(Andante con moto)

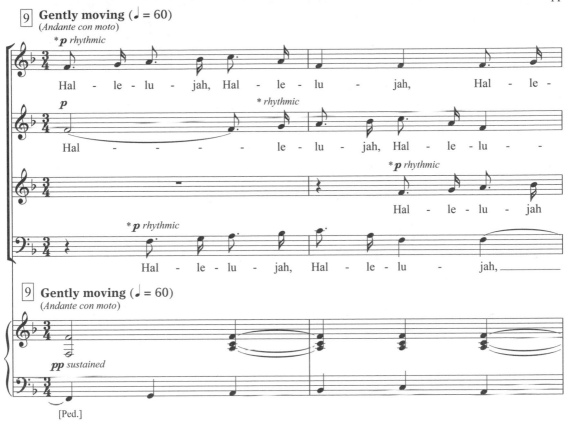

*♪.♪ *rhythmic* to be sung approximately as ♩♪

in - im - it - a - ble, and from the e - cho of the
ar - tist in - im - it - a - ble, and, and
ar - tist in - im - it - a - ble, and from the
in - im - it - a - ble,

hea - ven-ly harp in sweet-ness mag - ni - fi-cal and might -
from the e - cho, the e - cho of the hea - ven-ly harp,
e - cho of the hea - ven-ly harp in sweet - ness mag - ni - fi -
from the e - cho of the hea - ven-ly harp, mag-

attacca

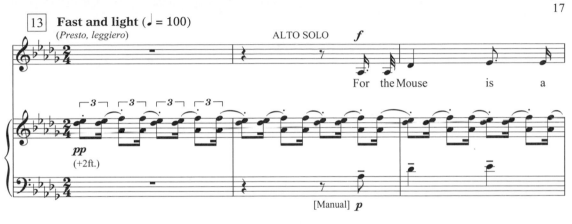

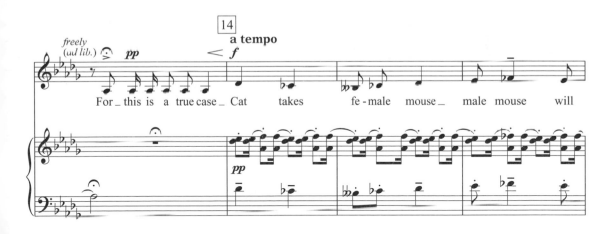

God and the root par-ries the ad-ver-sa-ry.

For there is a lan-guage of flowers. For flowers are pe-cu-liar-ly the po-e-try of Christ.

senza rit.

attacca

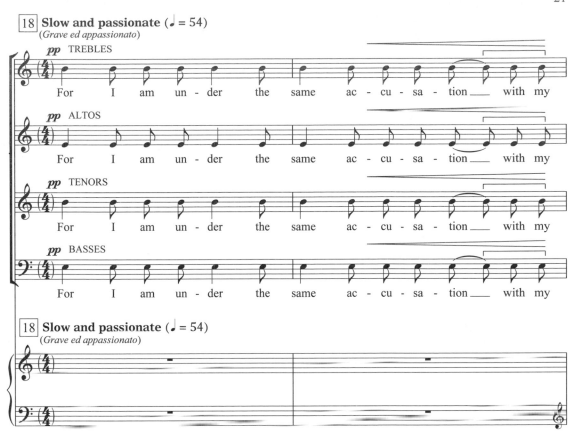

For the of-fi-cers of the peace are at va-ri-ance with me

For the of-fi-cers of the peace are at va-ri-ance with me

For the of-fi-cers of the peace are at va-ri-ance with me

For the of-fi-cers of the peace are at va-ri-ance with me

and the watch-man smites me with his staff.

and the watch-man smites me with his staff.

and the watch-man smites me with his staff.

and the watch-man smites me with his staff.

(Solo)

[Ped.]

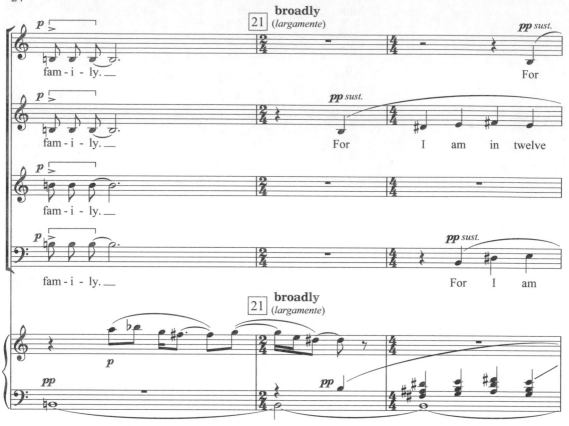

attacca

* *pronounce*: soote, moote.

28

For the Trum-pet of God is a bless - ed in-

For the Trum-pet of God is a bless - ed in-

For the Trum-pet of God is a bless - ed in-

For the Trum-pet of God is a bless - ed in-

cresc.

- tel - li - gence and so __ are all _____ the in - stru - ments in

- tel - li - gence __ and so __ are all _____ the in - stru - ments in

- tel - li - gence __ and all _____ the in - stru - ments in

- tel - li - gence __ and so __ are all _____ the in - stru - ments in

dim.

31 **Gently moving (as before)**
(*Andante con moto (come sopra)*)

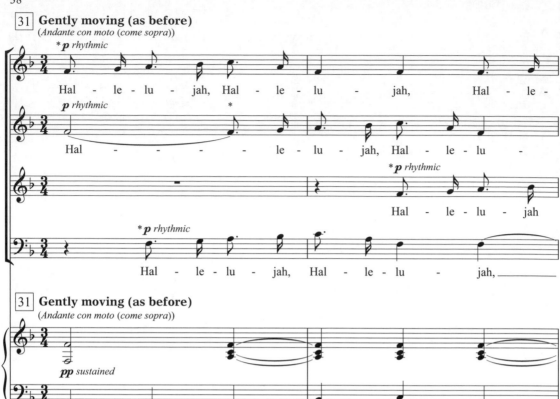

31 **Gently moving (as before)**
(*Andante con moto (come sopra)*)

*♪. ♪ *rhythmic* to be sung approximately as ♩ ♪

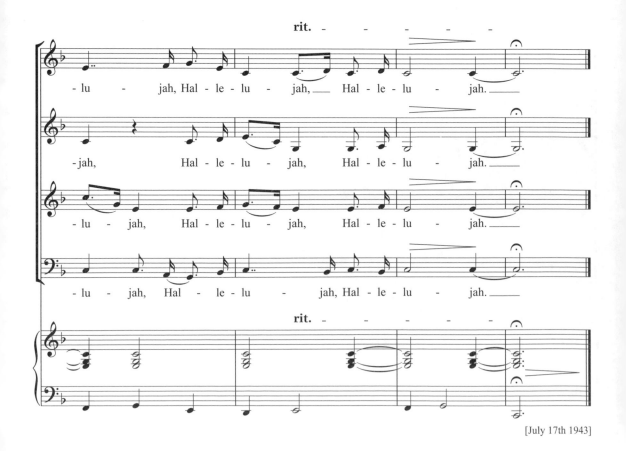

[July 17th 1943]

BENJAMIN BRITTEN was born in Lowestoft, Suffolk, on the east coast of England, on 22 November 1913. Although he was already composing vigorously as a child, he nonetheless felt the importance of some solid guidance and in 1928 turned to the composer Frank Bridge; two years later he went to the Royal College of Music in London, studying with Arthur Benjamin, Harold Samuel and John Ireland. While still a student, he wrote his 'official' Op. 1, the Sinfonietta for chamber ensemble, and the Phantasy Quartet for oboe and string trio, and in 1936 he composed *Our Hunting Fathers*, an ambitious song-cycle for soprano and orchestra, which confirmed Britten's virtuosic vocal and instrumental technique. He was already earning his living as a composer, having joined the GPO (Post Office) Film Unit the previous year; the collaboration he began there with the poet W. H. Auden was to prove an important one throughout his career.

Britten found himself in the United States at the outset of World War II and stayed there for three more years, returning to Britain in 1942. In America he produced a number of important works, among them the orchestral Sinfonia da Requiem, the song-cycle *Les Illuminations* for high voice and strings, and his Violin Concerto. With the opera *Paul Bunyan* he also made his first essay in a genre that would be particularly important to him.

Back in Britain, where as a conscientious objector he was excused military service, he began work on the piece that would establish him beyond question as the pre-eminent British composer of his generation – the opera *Peter Grimes*, premiered to an ecstatic reaction on 7 June 1945. The Young Person's Guide to the Orchestra: Variations and Fugue on a Theme of Purcell – a cornerstone of the orchestral repertoire – was first performed in the following year. Indeed, Britten now composed one major work after another, among them the operas *The Rape of Lucretia* (1946), *Albert Herring* (1947), *Billy Budd* (1951), *Gloriana* (1953), *The Turn of the Screw* (1954), *Noye's Fludde* (1957), *A Midsummer Night's Dream* (1960), *Owen Wingrave* (1970–71) and *Death in Venice* (1971–73); the Nocturne for tenor and orchestra (1958), the War Requiem (1961–62), a Cello Symphony (1963) for Rostropovich and his orchestral Suite on English Folk Tunes (1974).

Britten's importance in post-War British cultural life was enhanced by his founding of the English Opera Group in 1946 and the Aldeburgh Festival two years later. His career as a composer was matched by his outstanding ability as a performer: he was both a refined pianist and a spontaneous and fluent conductor – his Mozart was particularly highly esteemed. Britten's later career was clouded by bouts of ill-health, culminating in heart disease. He never fully recovered from open-heart surgery in 1973, and died on 4 December 1976, at the age of 63, a few months after being appointed a Life Peer, 'Baron Britten of Aldeburgh in the County of Suffolk'– the first composer ever to know that honor.